Canine Rhymes

Dog Titles By Mark Asher

All That Ails You
Humphrey Was Here
Miracle On Miravasa
A Day In Dogtown
Birdcall Morning
A Night At The Animal Shelter

Canine Rhymes

POEMS TO CELEBRATE
OUR FUREVER COMPANIONS

MARK J. ASHER

For Humphrey, Payton, and Reese

PREFACE

Those who have read my previous dog books might ask, "Poetry?" Well, believe or not, poetry isn't that far of a stretch for me. Back in my early 20s, I wrote lyrics to pop and R&B songs with my then brother-in-law. As you'll soon discover, my love of music is reflected in this collection in a couple of places. I've even included two parody lyrics to Beatles' songs.

The poems presented within this book are a mix of several themes: whimsical dog adventures, inspirational roles dogs play in our lives, turning points in a dog's journey, and dogs in historical settings. Some were ideas or images that have been floating around in my head for years, while others were spurred by stories that I read. Of course, a great deal of what comes out in my books is my experiences of sharing my life with dogs.

Working on this collection of dog poems has been pure bliss. It was a refreshing change to complete a piece of work rather quickly versus laboring over a novel for years. My hope is that the poems offer smiles, laughs, and recollections, as you spend time reading about one of the greatest gifts to humankind — dogs. Once you finish, if you have a favorite poem, I'd love to know. Drop me an email at mark@markjasher.com.

CONTENTS

EMBRACING THE UNFORESEEN

A middle-aged man named Blaine
Woke up to discover he was a Great Dane
At first, he was horrified and terribly confused
But he quickly realized he had new skills he could use

He had a wagging tail and a wet nose to sniff
He could run and play without feeling stiff
He chased squirrels in the park and fetched sticks in the lake
No longer concerned about his career, his stress began to abate

He loved the feeling of grass beneath his paws
He licked where he wanted just because
He ate his meals from a bowl and drank from a dish
He lived each moment without a single want or wish

In the middle of each perfectly precious day
Blaine curled up and slept the afternoon away
Unburdened by the troubles of man
He found happiness in the simplest things, as a
Great Dane can

A BRIGHT SPOT IN THE DARK

Sam the yellow Lab, with a wag in his tail
Visited young Chelsea, who was weak and frail
He leapt up on the bed and gave her a kiss
Chelsea's face lit up, as she felt a moment of bliss

Sam was a special dog, trained to bring cheer
To children facing challenges that were severe
He lay his head on her lap and let out a sigh
As if to say, "I'm here for you, don't be shy"

Chelsea reached out a hand and stroked his soft fur
Feeling a warmth and love that only a dog can stir
Sam licked her hand and let out a playful growl
Bringing a smile to Chelsea's face, as she let out a howl

All afternoon, the two laughed and played games
Reminding the young girl of her life before it changed
The miracle of a dog brightened Chelsea's day
And for a little while, her cancer seemed far, far away

HARLEY & GUINEVERE

Harley the Saint Bernard was a dog of great size
He lived with his family and was always their prize
But when they brought home a cat named Guinevere
Harley didn't like this new creature being near

He growled and he barked and he chased her about
He tried to scare her, no doubt
But Guinevere was a sly little thing
She always found a way to give Harley a sting

Harley was baffled, he couldn't understand
Why this little cat was always close at hand
But as the days went by and he watched her up close
He began to see for a feline she was better than most

He saw her purring as she lies in the sun
He saw her playing with a ball, just for fun
He saw the love and care his family gave her
And slowly but surely, his heart began to purr

Now Harley and Guinevere are the best of friends
Their bond is special and it will never end
They play and they cuddle and they snooze the day away
And Harley is glad he gave Guinevere a chance to stay

FIREPLACE FANTASIES

A dog lies by the fireplace on a cold winter's day
Dreaming of chasing a squirrel so full of play
The flames dance and flicker casting a warm glow
As the dog's tail thumps gently to and fro

Outside, the wind howls and the snow falls deep
But inside, all is warm and the dog's fast asleep
In his dreams, he runs through the fields and woods
Savoring his chance to capture the elusive goods

His paws pound the ground as he races ahead
His tongue lolls out as he bounds with glee, unfed
But alas, it is only a dream, as all dreams must end
And the dog awakens to the cold winter's wind

But still, he lies contentedly by the fire
Waiting for another squirrel to stir his desire
For though the winter's cold may bring freeze
The warmth of the hearth and his dreams appease

A DOG'S PLIGHT

Eight year old Sadie sits at the front of her cage
Scared and confused, she tries to gauge
What happened to bring her here
To this place of noise and fear

She remembers the family that gave her a chance
She has no idea why they changed their stance
But now she's back in this cold, lonely place
Her heart aches with sorrow, her spirit erased

She longs to be loved and to have a true home
To roam free and play, no longer alone
But for now, she waits, her head hung low
Hoping that someone special will show

She's a wonderful dog with a heart that's pure
She deserves a second chance, that's for sure
It's easy to take home something young and new
It's another to see a dog's life all the way through

So, when you see a dog at the front of its cage
Take a moment to stop, no matter it's condition or age
You never know the love that you might find
In the eyes of a dog left behind

THE BEAGLES HAVE LANDED

Three Beagles, Luna, Sally, and Ace
Set off on a journey through space
Their mission, to land on the moon
A place no dog had ever graced

The rocket soared through the sky
Leaving Earth far behind
The dogs looked cute in their space suits
As they got closer to their pursuit

Once they landed on the lunar surface
The dogs rushed out the door
Taking their first steps on the moon
They were excited to wander and explore

They sniffed around, taking in the vast territory
Cameras on their helmets recorded the story
Soon, the strange weightlessness of space
Set the dogs off on a goofy game of chase

Once they returned to Earth
The dogs were hailed as heroes
For their bravery and determination
And for keeping their mistakes to zero

So big ups for the three dog astronauts
Who made history that day
Their names will go down in the books
As the pups who paved the way

THE LABRADOORS

There's a hot new band of Labrador Retrievers
With music like you've never heard before
They go by the name The Labradoors
And their shows leave crowds begging for more

Jim, the lead singer, puts female fans into a fever
Ray, the keyboardist, is a clever sound weaver
Robby, the guitarist, knows just how to rock
John, the drummer, keeps the beat non-stop

With Jim's howls and Robby's riffs
Their audiences hardly get a chance to sit
Ray's organ solos are innovative and sharp
And John's tail drum sets the band apart

The Labradoors are a sight to see
Four dogs playing with kinetic energy
Their fans are always left in awe
And after the show, they all raise their paws

So if the Labradoors come to your town
Grab a friend and your favorite hound
Don't hesitate, pay whatever fee
To hear the best dog rock band in history

A PUP IS BORN

Rufus was just a tiny pup
Freshly born and full of love
His eyes were closed, his fur soft
A bundle of joy in a bright lit loft

He snuggled close to his momma's side
Feeling warm and safe and alive
He heard the sounds of his siblings' cries
But for now, he just wanted to close his eyes

As the day went on and the sun did rise
Rufus opened his eyes to a whole new surprise
He saw the light shining bright and bold
The start of his story was about to be told

Rufus wiggled his tail and let out a squeak
He nuzzled against his siblings, innocent and sweet
His nose and paws were a pinkish red
He followed his mother wherever she led

The humans looked on, filled with delight
The miracle of birth, a breathtaking sight
In new homes, the puppies' lives will soon begin
Bringing more joy than could ever be imagined

TAILWIND

In a classroom full of curious kids
An idea was born, a plan to rid
The town of power woes, once and for all
They'd harness the wags of dogs, big and small

With tails wagging fast, they'd generate gusts
To turn the turbines, it was a must
They drew up plans and made a pitch
To the town council, without a glitch

The council members were skeptical, but the kids were bold
They refused to quit trying until their plan was sold
Then they gathered every dog from near and far
And got to work to make their mark

The dogs obeyed, wagging their tails with glee
As the turbines turned, generating energy
The kids cheered and clapped, they had done it right
The town was powered through the day and night

The kids then decided to form a new entity
Appropriately called Tailwind Energy
The company gave each participating dog a stake
That was paid out in bones at a generous rate

A FUREVER GIFT

Abe was a sad and diffident boy, running out of hope
He desperately wanted a dog to help him cope
With the challenges of life and all its ups and downs
A furry companion to take on walks around the town

He begged and pleaded with his parents every day
For a dog to come and fill his life with play
Finally, they relented and brought home a pup
Abe was overjoyed, his heart filled with love

Auggie was the dog's name, a rambunctious little thing
He instantly took to Abe and was always on his wing
The boy vowed to train the dog well, to be the best
To follow commands and not beg like a pest

They started with the basics, sit and stay
Abe was patient as Auggie learned to obey
Then came the tricks, and Abe's favorite game
Fetch, where Auggie retrieved the ball again and again

Abe and Auggie bonded as the days went by
And Abe became more confident and less shy
Getting a dog was everything Abe had hoped for
Auggie eventually led him to a girl that he adored

The girl became a woman and then Abe's wife
He still reflects on how Auggie changed his life
Both of Abe's kids love dogs as deeply as him
His family has a Golden, a Lab, and two Min Pins

THE FIRST SNOW

I'm Finn the puppy, so fresh and bold
On my first snow day, a sight to behold
I leap and I bound through the powdery white
My tail wags with joy, I'm an adorable sight

My paws sink deep as I run through the drifts
My fur coat keeps me warm, a wintery gift
I chase the flakes falling through the air
My energy boundless, a pup without care

I tumble and roll, a blur of fur and snow
I'm frosty white from head to toe
I wish everyday was just like this
Filled with endless fun and wintery bliss

Look! A snowman with a carrot as a nose
I know a better place for that to go
Crunch, crunch, yum, yum
Can I have another one?

PRAYER FOR A SHELTER DOG

Old Rusty lies in his kennel
A faithful friend and loyal fella
Once a beloved pet, now cast aside
In this cold, sterile shelter he's forced to reside

His once glossy coat has grown thin and gray
His eyes are dim, he can't run and play
But still, he wags his tail with joy
Hoping for another chance to be a loving boy

He misses the days of belly rubs and treats
Riding to the dog park in the passenger seat
But now those days are just a distant memory
As he waits to be adopted again and set free

Sweet Rusty, old boy, don't lose hope
Your forever home is out there, you just gotta cope
Don't give up, don't lose faith
Someone soon will come and give you a warm embrace

Until then, Rusty, keep your head held high
Before you know it, you'll be bidding this place goodbye
Off to a new home where you're cared for and adored
No longer a shelter dog, but loved forever more

STEALING AWAY TO THE DOG PARK

Bonnie and Clyde were two mischievous pups
Who loved to cause a little stir
They were always up to something
Their curiosity couldn't be cured

One day, they had a crazy idea
A plan that was bold and new
They decided to steal their owner's car
And drive to the dog park to see their canine crew

Bonnie hopped into the driver's seat
And fiddled with the keys
She figured out how to start the car
And her and Clyde were off with ease

They drove down the street
Bonnie's ears flapped in the breeze
While Clyde looked beneath his seat
For treats and leftover food to eat

Once they reached the dog park
They were greeted with wags and barks
All the dogs ran up to meet them
As Bonnie and Clyde made their marks

But as they were having fun
They heard a loud siren sound
They looked up and saw the police
And their joy quickly died down

Their owner had been taking a daily nap
Waking up, she screamed, "Holy crap!"
Her car was tracked and the dogs were in trouble
Bonnie and Clyde were taken home on the double

Even though the dogs got a scolding
They didn't have any regret
The joy and adventure they had
Was worth their owner briefly being upset

LIBERTY ABOARD THE MAYFLOWER

Liberty, a noble dog, brave and true
Sailed with the Pilgrims and the Mayflower crew
Bound for a land unknown
A place where they could start anew

Through storms and rough seas
The dog stood tall and strong
Guiding the way for those aboard
Through the journey that was long

As the Mayflower reached the shore
And the Pilgrims stepped on land
Liberty was there with them
With a wagging tail, ready to make a stand

For this dog knew the journey
Was not just for man alone
But for all creatures, great and small
Who sought a new home

So as the Pilgrims built their homes
And started a life in the New World
Liberty was by their side
A faithful and loyal friend, unfurled

Through all the trials and struggles
Liberty remained a constant guide
Bringing love and loyalty
To those who came from far and wide

And as the years went by
And the Pilgrims' story was told
The dog was remembered
As a great patriot and noble soul

FOREVER IN MY HEART

Gone too soon, dear friend of mine
With you there never could be enough time
Still, I wait for you to bound up beside me
And soothe this grief that's deep inside me

Though you're gone, you'll never be forgotten
Your love and loyalty, a bond unbroken
You brought joy to every single day
In your absence, I'll find a way

To honor you and all you've meant
A faithful companion, Heaven sent
I'll hold you close, deep in my heart
I promise we'll never be far apart

So, rest in peace, my furever friend
Until we meet again, my love will never end

A CANINE LIFELINE

Rosie is a special dog
She helps the blind see
Every day is an adventure
As she guides Claire with glee

She wakes up bright and early
Ready to start the day
She stretches and wags her tail
She's eager to get on her way

Next, it's time to get dressed
Rosie wears her special vest
That lets everyone know
She's a guide dog with a special role

She leads Claire through the city
Navigating streets and crowds
She makes sure they stay safe
When things get chaotic and loud

She takes her to the store
The park, and everywhere Claire needs
She is a constant companion
A guide, a friend indeed

She listens to Claire's commands
And helps her with their tasks
She is her faithful partner
And love and treats are all she asks

So, here's to Rosie
A guide dog and an angel too
She allows Claire to see the world
And do things she otherwise couldn't do

BENEATH THE TABLE

Garvey the English bulldog
Loving, loyal, and cute
Sits beneath the kitchen table
Eagerly waiting for his due

With a keen sense of smell
And a gleam in his eye
He watches for falling scraps
And never lets them pass him by

He's the family's faithful friend
And the kitchen's resident clown
He brings joy and laughter
Whenever he's around

So, if you see a bulldog
Lazing beneath the kitchen table
Say hello to Garvey
And give him pets if you are able

A CANINE'S CRAVING

The dog sits and waits with bated breath
Watching her owner to see what's next
Eyes fixed on the treats with an intense gaze
The seconds pass like days

At last the treat is hers and she devours it
She puts her nose on the floor and scours it
Finally looking up, she licks her lips and gives a wag
Thankful for the satisfaction from the crinkly bag

A BRIDGE TO BRIGHTER DAYS

I am a service dog named Lexi
Trained to help and comfort, my job is to be
A constant presence and calming force
For a veteran who struggles to stay the course

I wake up every day, ready to serve
To be by Megan's side, to help her preserve
Her sanity, her peace of mind
To leave the horrors of the past behind

I stay close to her wherever we are
Ready to help, to heal the scar
That war has left deep inside
I am her rock, her faithful guide

I do tasks, big and small
To ease her burden, to help her stand tall
I fetch, I carry, I open doors
I am her eyes and ears and so much more

Eventually, Megan will greet a brighter day
When the joy of living outweighs the pain
But until then, I'll do whatever it takes
To ease her trauma, stress, and heartache

TAIL-WAGGING TUNES

Melody, the Golden Retriever
A joyful pup with a wagging tail
Whenever her owner strums his guitar
Melody can't help but wail

She dances to the music's beat
Her paws moving left and right
Her face is filled with pure delight
It's quite an adorable sight

Her owner launches into an upbeat song
And Melody begins to howl along
They're an awesome band of two
That is original through and through

So, if you see a Golden Retriever
Dancing to the sound of a guitar
You'll know it's Melody
The most musical pup by far

SHE RUBS ME
SUNG TO THE BEATLES "SHE LOVES YOU"

She rubs me, yeah, yeah, yeah
She rubs me, yeah, yeah, yeah
She loves me, yeah, yeah, yeah, yeah

I was rotting in a cage
Running out of time
Waiting endlessly
For someone sweet and kind

Then she rubbed me
And I'm doing a wiggle wag
She loved me
And I'm no longer sad (howl instead of ooh)

Life behind bars
You know it's a drag
Sleeping on an old bed
That seriously sags

But then rubbed me
And I'm doing a wiggle wag
She loved me
And I'm no longer sad (howl instead of ooh)

She rubs me, yeah, yeah, yeah
She loves me, yeah, yeah, yeah
And with breath like mine
You know I'm really glad

To humans everywhere
With a heart and a bone
There's nothing like the joy
Of giving a dog a new home

She rubs me, yeah, yeah, yeah
She loves me, yeah, yeah, yeah
And with breath like mine
You know I'm really glad

And with breath like mine
You know that can't be bad
And with breath like mine
You know I'm really glad

Yeah, yeah, yeah
Yeah, yeah, yeah, yeah

RESCUE DOG
SUNG TO THE BEATLES "NOWHERE MAN"

He's a large furry mutt
With a strange haircut
And he chews on everything he sees

Doesn't know sit from stand
Does whatever he has planned
Some days I wonder if he's stolen my sanity
Rescue dog, please listen
You know you should be sittin'
Rescue dog, the treats you crave are in my commands

Don't cop an attitude
Remember who rescued you
And just be happy you're no longer in the pound.
Rescue dog, won't you listen
You don't know what you're missin'
Rescue dog, the treats you crave are in my commands

We gave our mutt the name Fred
In time he listened to what we said
Now he looks at us with love in his eyes
Rescue dog, thanks for listening
Your teeth and coat are glistening

Rescue dog, you're better than any show dog I know

Fred's the best rescue pooch
He's as smart as he is cute
I hope he lives a long, long time
I hope he lives a long, long time
I hope he lives a long, long time

SITTING PRETTY

Training your dog can be fun
But first you need to know how it's done
To teach your furry friend to sit
It'll take just a little bit

Hold a treat in your hand
Show it to your dog, they'll understand
Slowly move the treat up and over their head
As they look up, they'll sit instead

As soon as they do, say "Good sit!"
And give them the treat, that's it
With practice and patience your dog will learn
When they listen, there are treats to be earned

IN DOG WE TRUST

Theodore the dog was a special pup
With an expressive face you couldn't help but love
He was energetic and smart and always up for a game
But little did anyone know, he had a higher aim

Theodore dreamed of a world where every dog was free
Where they could run and play and live happily
He wanted to abolish animal shelters
And turn the oval office into the shape of a bone
So, he set his sights on the White House from his
owner's home

The campaign was tough, with many a foe
But Theodore never wavered, he was gung ho
He barked and he yipped and kept his spirits high
Before long, the votes were in and the results didn't lie

Theodore the dog, against all odds
Had become the leader of the land and the nation was awed
He worked like a dog to keep the promises he made
And he never golfed, not even for one day

So, here's to Theodore, a dog who dared to dream
He proved anything is possible when you assemble a loyal team
He will always be remembered as the canine in chief
Who brought about happiness and gave us all relief

A WARM HEART IN A COLD WORLD

An old man on a record cold, snowy day
Lived alone in the country, far away
From the warmth and the bustle of the city's embrace
He faced the storm with a stoic grace

The power had gone out in his old, tiny house
So he huddled by the fire, quiet as a mouse
Away from the comforts of the world outside
He was content to simply reside

His kids tried to reach him on the phone
But the lines were down, so he was on his own
He did, however, have a sweet and loyal mutt
With Ernest by his side, the old man would buckle up

Through the blizzard and the seemingly endless night
He clung to his dog with all his might
And when the dawn finally broke through the clouds
He knew that he had made it through somehow

The old man on the coldest, snowiest day
Lived to see another sunrise in his own way
He was strong, he was brave, he was true
And he had Ernest to see him through

WAITING FOR YOU KNOW WHO

A dog and a cat sit and wait
For their owner to come home through the gate
The dog wags his tail and pants with glee
While the cat twitches her tail lazily

The dog speaks first, "I love to run and play
Fetching sticks is my favorite game
But when my owner comes home at night
I'm always ready to cuddle and snuggle tight"

The cat responds with a purr and a nod
"I prefer to relax and take things slow
But I do enjoy a good game of chase
Especially when it's with a dangling string or lace"

The dog tilts his head and asks with curiosity
"Don't you get lonely, waiting around aimlessly?
Don't you miss your owner's company?"

The cat pauses and then says casually
"I do enjoy my solitude and quiet time
But I always look forward to seeing my owner again
I consider her to be a very special friend"

The dog nods in understanding and agrees
"Yes, there's nothing quite like the bond we share
With our owner, who loves and cares
No matter if we're a dog or a cat, it's a gift beyond
compare"

A HEALING PRESENCE

I am Jofi, Sigmund Freud's loyal chow
You can find me curled up on the couch
Listening to Freud's patients speak
Of their sorrows, their joys, and the secrets they keep

I am just a simple dog, but I know
Freud's words bring healing to those who are in woe
I watch him work, his brow furrowed in thought
As he helps his patients feel less distraught

When the hour grows late, I start to yawn
It's a signal to Freud that it's time to move on
To the next patient, to the next case
Hoping they too will leave in a better place

So, I'll continue to sit and listen and yawn
In Freud's therapy sessions, until the day is gone
For I am Jofi, Freud's loyal chow
And I am here to help any way that I know how

A SIGHT TO BEHOLD

A weary animal shelter worker
Comes to work each day
To care for all the creatures
That are turned in or found as strays

One day shortly after she arrived
She saw a shocking and unusual sight
In the cages where the dogs should be
Were animal abusers filled with fright

She grinned from ear to ear
As she scanned the cages front to rear
For she knew that justice had been served
And the heartless bastards got what they deserved

But just as the world seemed right and just
From an open window, she felt a strong gust
She was awakened from her pleasant dream
And her soul let out a helpless scream

BONDING THROUGH OBSTACLES

I love to run and jump and play
Agility is my favorite way
To show my skills and have some fun
With my owner and best friend, my number one

We race through tunnels, jump over walls
Weave through poles, we conquer all
The obstacles that come our way
Together, we make a great team, I must say

My tail wags with pure delight
As we work together with all our might
I trust my owner with all my heart
We're always in sync, never apart

Agility is how we get our fill
You might call it our happy pill
To compete hard and win is our mission
But agility is about camaraderie and competition

THE LAST DAYS OF LOU GEHRIG

The last days of Lou Gehrig's life were filled with pain
His body ravaged by a disease that couldn't be tamed
But through it all, there was one constant by his side
A feisty little dog named Yankee, Lou's loyal pride

Eleanor, Lou's wife, did not share the same affection
For the small and scrappy dog, she had no connection
But Lou loved Yankee with all of his heart
The dog was a great comfort, and the two were
never apart

As Lou's time on earth came to a close
Eleanor made a decision everyone opposed
She asked the vet to put the dog down, to end its life
But the vet had a conscience and denied Lou's wife

He refused to euthanize a healthy dog, no matter what
Eleanor said
He knew it was wrong and he wouldn't go ahead
Eventually, Yankee found a home where he was loved
And Lou was smiling down from Heaven above

A BOX FULL OF LOVE

I lie beneath the tree, my first Christmas here
In my new home, filled with love and cheer
A box with my name is topped with a big bow
I wonder what's inside, I'm sniffing to know

I hope it's treats and toys that are fun
I'll eat and play until the day is done
But for now, I'll close my eyes and try to sleep
I'll count squirrels instead of sheep

Soon, I wake to the sound of my family's laughter
They scoop me up and say "Merry Christmas, Jasper!"
I return to my box and my tail starts to wag
Suddenly, I'm showered with gifts that I quickly snag

My first Christmas is one I'll always remember
I can hardly wait for next December
But being part of a family beats anything that's edible
They've made this foster fail feel special
and unforgettable

A STRAY DOG'S
CHRISTMAS MIRACLE

A stray dog wanders the streets at night
During the holiday season, cold and bright
She's tired and hungry, feeling alone
But then she finds a Nativity scene, a place to call home

She curls up inside the stable, warm and snug
Mother Mary makes room with a gentle nudge
The stray dog closes her eyes, and twitches as she dreams
A drunk man walks by and mumbles, "Is that what
it seems?"

Hours later, the dog gives birth by the manger
As the baby Jesus watches, a welcome stranger
The mother and her pups are surrounded by
love and light
As the holiday spirit carries them through the night

When morning comes and the sun rises on Christmas Day
Visitors behold the sight inside the straw-lined display
The stray dog and her puppies, they'll always be blessed
For they found a home in the Nativity scene's nest

RETIREMENT OF A K-9 HERO

Kyro, my faithful K-9 partner
Ten years of service, we've been through it all
From chasing down suspects to sniffing out drugs
You've always been there, standing tall

Your keen sense of smell and lightning-fast speed
Have helped us keep the streets safe and secure
I've always relied on your bravery and strength
Of your dedication, I've always been sure

But now it's time for you to retire
To rest and enjoy the fruits of your labor
I'll never forget all the adventures we've had
I served with the fiercest crime crusader

So let me hug you and give you one more bone
Before you go off to your new home
Kyro, I'll cherish the memories of our time together
And I'll carry your spirit in my heart forever

DISCOVERING DOGTOWN

Once there was a young boy named Zach
Who lived in a resort town called Tamarack
He was curious and shy and one day he strayed
Beyond the borders of his home and far away

Through thick woods, he took in sights and sounds
Until he ended up in a strange and wondrous town
A place filled with dogs as far as the eye could see
Zach saw things he never would have believed

There were dogs behind the wheels of cars
There were dogs in restaurants and in bars
There were dogs gathered in the town's square
Where a machine was tossing bones in the air

The boy was enthralled and he decided to stay
To explore this lively and unique place
He spent his time visiting with canines of every kind
He couldn't remember when he had such a good time

But as the days went by, Zach began to miss
His parents, his neighbors, and Jamie, his big sis
So with a heavy heart, he turned and walked away
Leaving Dogtown behind, but vowing to return one day

Zach suddenly woke up and looked around confused
His father, by his side, told him to put on his shoes
The boy began to tell his dad where he had been
His father smiled and said, "You've been
dreaming again."

But that's not the end of this story
Zach soon got a shelter dog named Cory
His parents were tired of his endless pleading
So on a dog, they finally ended up conceding

HOPE AMID THE HEARTBREAK

Major General Garrison stood on Omaha's shore
A few days after D-Day's bloody war
He came upon a Brittany Spaniel, alone and afraid
The dog followed him to where he and his men stayed

The dog never left the General's sight
He was a faithful companion, a joy and a delight
The war raged on, but the dog remained
A constant presence through the conflict's pain

The days turned to months and the war drew to a close
Sadly, the General knew he had to let the dog go
It was against military rules to bring him home
No matter how his love for the dog had grown

The soldiers could see that their leader was blue
But they knew there was something they could do
They smuggled the dog in a duffel bag bound for home
On the journey, he was cared for and given lots of bones

Major General Garrison had tears in his eyes
When he learned of his soldiers' surprise
The Brittany Spaniel, now known as Lucky
Went home with the General to a farm in Kentucky

FROM JEALOUSY TO JOY

Lucy, our chocolate Lab
Was once the center of our world
She brought us joy and love
A constant presence, a loyal girl

But then one day our lives changed forever
Our family grew by two
Twin girls, so small and sweet
They made our family complete

But Lucy saw things differently
She was confused and filled with jealousy
How could these tiny, whiny humans take
A loyal and loving dog's place?

But as the days went by
Lucy learned to love the girls
She watched them grow and change
And made them part of her world

Now, Lucy is the big sister
A protector and a guide
She plays with the girls day and night
And is always by their side

Lucy's embrace of our unexpected surprise
Still brings tears to this mother's eyes
Some angels choose fur instead of wings
Lucy is proof with all the love she brings

ON THE SCENT OF TRUTH

I am the nose that knows no bounds
The tracking bloodhound that always astounds
With my keen sense of smell and tireless pace
I am the one they call for a crucial case

Whether it's a missing person or a suspect on the run
I use my dogged determination to get the job done
I am a faithful partner to those in blue
Dedicated to serving and protecting, it's what I do

TALL AND SMALL

Once, an elephant and a tiny dog
Were strangers, nothing more
But one fateful day, they met
And a change was in store

The elephant was tall and grand
His trunk reaching high in the air
The dog was small and skittish
And she didn't have any hair

The two couldn't have been more different
Their size, their shape, their hue
But as they spent more time together
They became a bonded team of two

The dog liked to curl up on the elephant and lay
Bathing in the glorious sunshine all day
The elephant liked when the dog massaged his back
Every time she chased after a fly or a gnat

And so it was that an elephant and a dog
Became the very best of friends
Their differences no longer mattered
On each other they came to depend

The elephant and the tiny dog paved the way
With the unique connection that they made
They've shown that color, shape, and size
Like all beauty, is in the beholder's eyes

A PAIR BEYOND COMPARE

The dog and sea lion swam in the ocean
Toward a bright green ball set in motion
The sea lion, sleek and agile in the waves
The dog, bounding with energy, eager to play

As they chased the ball, their joy was plain to see
The dog barking, the sea lion barking back with glee
The two of them together caused quite a stir
Not every day did something like this occur

When both were tired and had given their best
The dog lay his head on the sea lion's chest
Their bond formed by the joy of play
A precious sight on a summer day

AN END TO INSANITY

Catherine sat with her dog Spencer in the dark
Holding him close, she could feel his beating heart
Constant explosions outside sounded like war
Spencer was trembling, freighted to his core

The dog broke free from Catherine's embrace
Scurrying to find a less terrifying place
Catherine found her dog shaking in the bath tub
She squeezed beside him and gave him gentle rubs

The hours went by and the noise did not abate
Poor Spencer continued to whimper and shake
Catherine looked angrily toward the sky and asked why
There was so much commotion on the 3rd of July

She thought about frightened animals everywhere
And closed her eyes and offered up a prayer
Then she wondered, what would it hurt
If the country enforced silent fireworks?

NOTE FROM THE AUTHOR

If you enter "dog book" in Amazon's search bar, the website returns a list of more than 100,000 titles. That's stiff competition no matter how good a book you've written! So, I have a favor to ask. If you enjoyed *Canine Rhymes*, and you know of another dog lover who would as well, please spread the word. If you'd be willing to post a review on Amazon or Goodreads, I'd be grateful. Thank you for reading one of my books and for your help!

All Good Things,
Mark J. Asher
www.MarkAsher.com

SPECIAL OFFER!

Purchase another copy of CANINE RHYMES for yourself or as a gift and save $5.00. Simply enter the discount code WAG at check out on **www.MarkAsher.com**. Along with your signed copy, you'll also receive a FREE die cut dog sticker!

all that ails you

The Adventures of a Canine Caregiver

A NOVEL BY
MARK J. ASHER

ALL THAT AILS YOU

Narrated by a rescue dog that ends up in a home for seniors, *All That Ails You* has over 600 five-star reviews on Amazon.

"The reader won't easily forget hard-working Wrigley, a dog who gives his whole heart to bringing out the best in people."
— *Susan Wilson, author of NY Times Bestseller, One Good Dog*

"Beautifully written. It is a book that will make you smile, laugh, cry and hug and kiss your own dog!"
— *Melissa A. Southard*

"Mark J. Asher has the writing talent of a human and the soul of a dog. Never did I think I could read a book narrated by a dog and be so captivated by it."
— *Mary Stephenson*

Made in the USA
Monee, IL
06 November 2024

69403346R00073